What I Love

What I Love

Poems of Green Forest

Written by Lotta Suter

Illustrations by Elizabeth Auer

Beinn Ard Publishing

Beinn Ard Publishing
Hollis, New Hampshire 03049
www.beinnard.com

These poems are works of fiction. All the characters and events portrayed in this book are fictitious, and any resemblance to real people or events is purely coincidental.

ISBN 978-1-889314-51-8 (hardcover)
ISBN 978-1-889314-52-5 (paperback)
ISBN 978-1-889314-53-2 (eBook)

Library of Congress Control Number: 2015949512

First edition 2015.

Printed in the United States of America

For Anja and Lucia

and all children and grandchildren

Contents

What I Love

How It All Began

How It All Began

How did it all begin
the sun, the moon, the earth, the sky?
Tell me, Wise Owl,
do you know why
our day and night,
dark and light,
hill and dale,
ant and whale
came about?
I try to answer and I fail.

Why is there each year a spring
a summer, fall and winter?
Tell me, Wise Owl,
how did the seasons enter
into the world we know?
Why do winds blow
and rivers flow?
Why does it snow
on big black Crow?
Please tell me if you know!

Why does Family Fox
eat birds and mice?
Tell me, Wise Owl,
I think that is not nice.
Why do animals and people die?
You must tell me why!
And also: how are babies born,
do they grow from a tiny corn?
Why do we laugh, why do we weep?
Teach me, Owl, your wisdom's deep.

How did it all begin
the sun, the moon, the earth, the sky?
Tell me, Wise Owl,
do you know why
our day and night,
dark and light,
hill and dale,
ant and whale
came about?
I'm sure you own the tale!

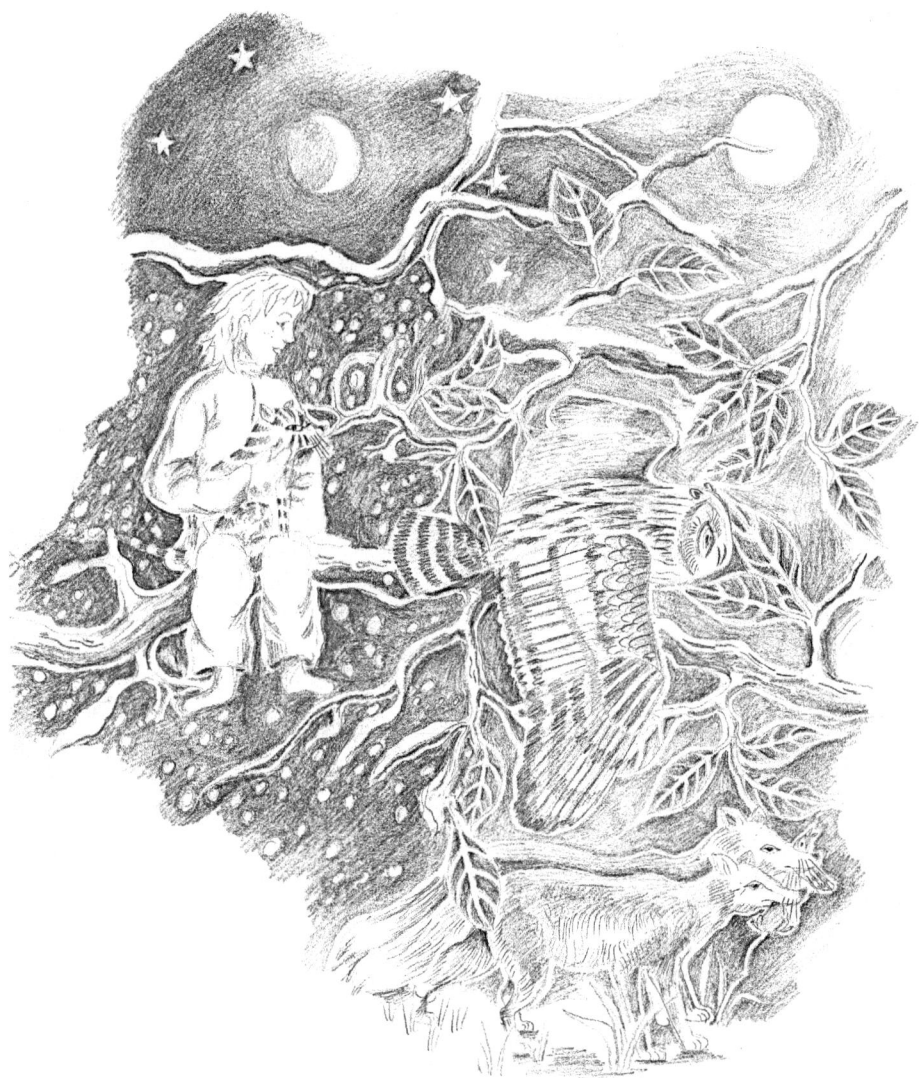

Stepping Stones

I like to skip from stone to stile
along our little brook.
I see big rivers underfoot – and look,
is that a crocodile?

I like to skip from stone to stile
surviving in the wild,
brave and heroic - no mere child! -
and hollering all the while.

I like to skip from stone to stile
until it's time to go back home
and I get tired of conning alone
there on my splendid Nile.

I skip away from stile and stone
the stream becomes a rill
and all my beasts despite their skill
in a nick of time are gone.

Spring River

Wait,
I hear some water gurgling
under its coat of ice and snow.
Rags, our little brook *does* flow!
A mere trickle from the well
soon now will swell
again, and grow its burbling.
Then all is well.

Flower Children

When ice and snow are melting
and the days grow long and light
I wish I were a worm
wriggling down and down and down
to watch how Mother Earth so gently
wakes her sleeping flower children.

I would like to be there
when the florets rub their starry eyes
and stretch and yawn,
throw off their leafy comforters
and watch expectantly
for what's to come.

Mother Earth greets every child
with a big smile, a tender touch
and shows them to the place
where she's laid out
the brand-new clothes
she sewed in long dark winter hours.

Poppy-red displays this dress,
Lavender blue another
Fuchsia here and purple there
pink for the Rose or Azalea
a greenish white for Snowdrop's robe
bright yellow for Forsythia.

The flower children don their frocks
some help the very young
button their coats,
and lace their shoes,
fasten their gay barrettes
and smooth out crinkles and wrinkles.

Then Mother Earth calls all her babes
by name and gives each one a kiss
she lines them up
to wait their turn
for rising to the warmth, the light,
making spring bloom and blossom.

Were I an earthworm I could see
the preparations down below.
But I am not and so I wait – up here!
impatiently! –
for liverleaf and daffodil
to lead the proud procession
of flowery fragrance
and flamboyant beauty.

Rags'
Rhyme

In spring
birds sing
flowers grow
you know –
that kind of thing.

A New Song

Before I open my eyes
I hear a songbird sing
I have not heard before.
The new song speaks of days
to come, of spring,
of brilliant joy and more.

I lie in bed and listen well
to Song Sparrow's chirp.
The bird is beaming with delight,
his chest has swelled
and he has stirred
my own heart to take flight.

The Fairy House

Today, in spring's first light
I've built a fairy house under the tree.
I hoped some fairies might
come by and see
the beauty of this tiny cot
and the very special things I brought:
a piece of shiny fabric for the floor
a silvery bell hung on the door
acorn cups and plates of bark
a glow fly even for the dark.
It is a splendid little house
for a fabulous fairy –
or a fabulous mouse.

Just Pretend

Pretend
I am a princess and Rags a unicorn.
We have umpteen adventures
in lands far and forlorn.

We meet monsters and dragons
and we conquer them all.
That is: *he* does, says Raggyns
(but that is just pretend!).

Always a Cat

Sometimes Ailinn asks me what
I would most like to be.
Well, I'll always be a cat
- what else? –
a cat, that's me!

Opposite Day

Cold is hot
big is small
what is, is not
and naught is all
I love opposite day!

I am old
Mom is a child
Rags the cat does as he's told
and Dad, Dad just runs wild
I love opposite day!

Rivers flow from mouth to spring
things fall upwards in the sky
Otter and Groundhog have grown wings
I am you and you are I
I love opposite day!

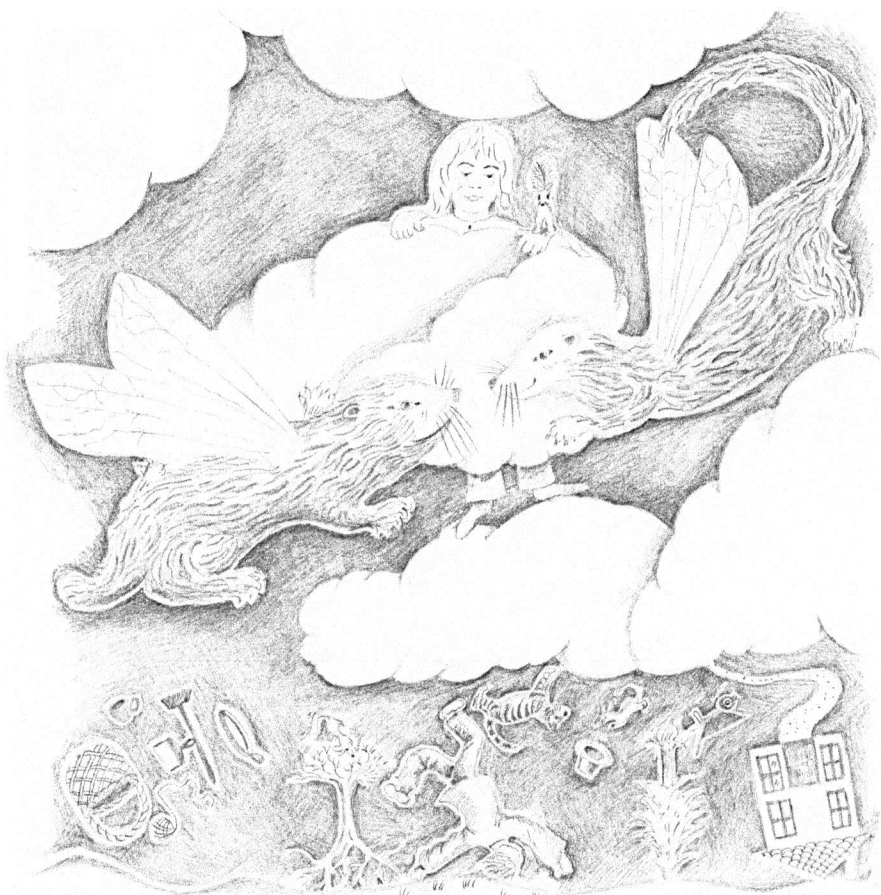

On the Mountain

I like to climb a mountain
pass meadow, forest, rock
and then a clear spring fountain
before I stand on top
of everything and grow so tall
(and the world below me is so small).
After my moment on this throne
alone
I go back down where I belong.
My friends have been waiting
                              all along!

My Kind of Fun

Paint a Rock

I paint on rock
a bear, a deer,
a flock of geese.

These ones go first
when sunbeams now
burst through the clouds

and brightly fall
upon my rock and
all its watery beasts.

Sun slurps them dry.
Why! that makes room
for different creatures.

My Kind of Fun

To lie in the sun, to stretch and yawn -
that is exactly my kind of fun!
Not Ailinn's though.
She is up and about,
hustling and bustling,
and here comes the shout:
"Raggyns come,
let's visit our Friend Otter!"
Don't like him,
don't want to,
don't slide in the water.
"Come on, Rags,
we will have so much fun!"
I guess, I'll go with her
(I *do* miss however
my snooze in the sun).

At the Pond

Quite ordinary is my pond -
but I found it!
And I am very fond
of my pond and all around it.

I like the shades and colors of my pond,
the ever changing water
and the trees and woods beyond,
I like all animals (and Otter!).

Have you ever seen a pond so clear,
so green, so blue, so fair?
So grey, so white, so sheer,
so calm, or now and then
so rippled by the air?

On foggy days the pond's at rest
in a silky gossamer cot
until one sunray on its quest
finds just that perfect spot.

The water comes alive with light
the pond is a golden mirror
that makes me and the day quite right
and brings happiness nearer.

Fish Wish

I wish
I were a fish
in a clear cool pond.
I'd swim around
in the swirls the sun
has spun
in the water and on the ground.
I'd play hide and seek
under a rock
and then I'd peek:
Is no one around?
Not even another fish?
I do wish....

Finding the Berry Patch

When summer reaches our Forest
and enters in its darkest crooks,
when trees glow green and all the brooks
glitter and twinkle and dazzle at their best
then Rags and I, we wander.

When the days grow bright and long
we explore each path, climb many a tree,
we talk to Dragonfly and then to Mrs. Bee,
and she tells us we should wander on
and look for that big clearing yonder.

Rags runs ahead, looks for a mark,
we find the glade and we are merry
because it's red and fragrant, full with berry
I pick and pick to fill my basket made of bark
and I don't hear the sudden thunder.

Rags warns of rain, he doesn't like the water.
We hurry to find shelter with some friends.
And that is how our berry-story ends:
Happy, because we have met Otter
(and he made us tasty Berry-Plunder).

Pick and Peck

I am standing in the bushes
picking berries into bowls.
Beneath me the chickens
keep pecking
at my raspberry red toes.

Chicken-Monster

Neighbor's chickens in our garden
look for worms.
Peck, peck, peck - pick and peck.
We like the chickens very much.

Last week pottering in our garden
we saw a worm.
Moist big fat shiny vermiform.
We liked the creature very much.

Now what
if the chickens find the big fat worm?

Mother opens the door and
Tch, tch, you chicken folk,
tch, tch, tch… Off you go!

"Don't!" I say to my mother,
"Don't scare the birds.
To them you are a monster!"

"And what about the worm?"
Mother asks. I say
"It would surely see
the chicken's monstrous beak
and hide away – wouldn't it?"

Father Fox

I saw the bright red brush of Father Fox
moving slyly through the wood
in search of prey to feed his cubs.
I guess that's good?

Brother Rabbit

I'd play tag with Brother Rabbit
If only I could

                   grab

                                 it.

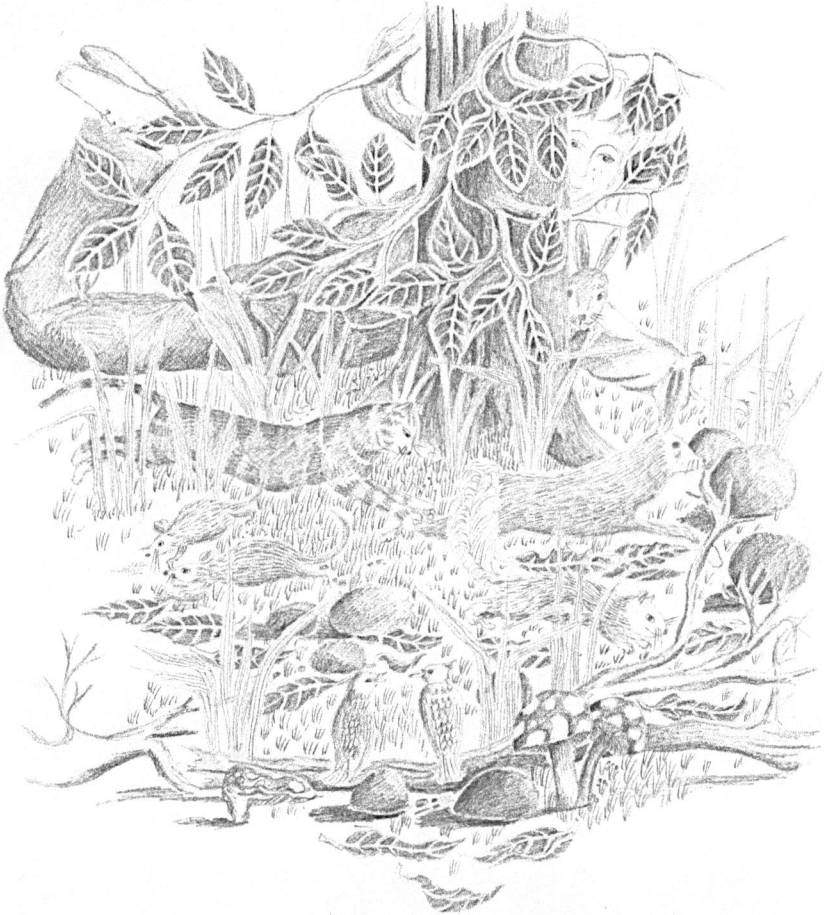

Beach Day

Planted
in the sand
these things:
a tree
a cloth
a book
a shoe.
Still life
stranded.
Above,
the wings
of dreams,
and clouds
of iridescent hue.

Shooting Star

When I see a shooting star,
can it hear me from afar,
the wish I send into the night
towards its fast vanishing light?

I do not ask for a great treasure
just for a bit of summer leisure
so that my friends and I
can go out and play.

Happiness

Happiness - a lazy afternoon
stuck in midsummer dream
time supended
the world without a care
a lightness of heart
still there.

Wanderlust

Tea With Otter

I like to visit Otter,
he's such a pleasant friend,
serves us toast with butter
and jams of every kind.

His house is small but cozy
just big enough for Rags and me.
My cheeks get hot and rosy
when he serves us ginger tea.

And all the while he chatters
and tells us many a tale
of everything that matters
in our little vale.

I'm fond of tea with Otter
he is such a good host.
And when he puffs and putters
I do like him the most.

Wanderlust

When the geese call to each other,
I would like to fly with them to foreign lands
I would like that.
When Father Bear tells me of olden times,
I would like to travel far into the past
I would like that.
When Grandma Groundhog tells me stories,
I would like to live in them completely
I would like that.
When Squirrel leaps from branch to branch,
I would like to bounce and jump as well
I would like that.
When Grey Wolf prowls at night, in moonlight
I would like to be part of the mystery
I would like that.
When Friend Otter dives and laughs all day,
I would like to be a member of his family
I would like that.

When Mom and Dad sit down for dinner
I like to join them
and feel wholeheartedly at home
I really like that.

Sea of Sadness

A child like me does know grey days -
no colors to hold on to,
mute days - no voices loud and clear,
empty days - no place to be.

On these lost days
I'm sailing on a sea of sadness.
No land, no dove
no olive branch in sight.

Yet grey days too
are veiled by gentle nights
with gentle darkness,
gentle rest.

And then again
I'm landing safely
on the shore of childhood,
hoping for tomorrow and what's in store.

Time's a Cat

Time's a stealthy cat like
Raggyns, stretching lazily
in the warm steady sun,
relaxed he is–
closing his eyes in pleasure
only now and then a twitch of tail

And then again
Raggyns looks up
alert and ready to rush off.
A mouse? A bird?
A barking dog?
A dry leaf dancing in the wind?

When you sit and read
or knit and dream
Rags will come to you
and settle in your lap
and purr you kindly
to your peace of mind…

...If you however
try to hold the cat
he'll show his claws
and disappear
in some dark corner.
Or he leaves the house.

Time and again
Rags comes and goes
at his own will.
No one so far has mastered
to have him curl up and unfurl
upon request.

Seeing in the Dark

I'm Raggyns the cat,
I can see in the dark
and that -
is not all!
I can hiss
I can scratch
and I jump off the wall.

But mostly I lie
stretched out in the sun
above me the sky
where the birds fly.
I twitch
I blink
I open one eye.

My eyes are bright yellow
and sharp as a dart.
I am the fellow
who sees in the dark -
that is, when I want to
or I'm (nicely) asked.

Carrying Burdens

I've met Auntie Ant today
as she was hurrying on her track.
"How are you?" I have asked her,
"what is the burden on your back?"
"I am quite well", she said politely,
and "carrying burdens is my lot."
"Yes, you are a busy worker" I replied,
"but can't you tell me what you've got?"
"Oh no, no, no", dear Auntie said,
"I do not need to know
the details of my daily toil,
the what and when and how.
I do my work and am content
I live my life and do not doubt
that somehow all of it makes sense
and someone somewhere knows about."

River Journey

We visit our river every day,
Rags is lapping water and I've come to play.
It's just a little brook
winding through Green Forest,
its chutes and rapids are awfully modest –
and yet each droplet of that stream
travels worlds like in a dream.
The water runs from springs up high
over rough cascades all the way
down to woodland, meadow, pond,
to bigger lakes and well beyond
to join large rivers and then flee
from damming levees to the Sea.
Yet in the ocean, it will not stay,
it aims for higher things and seeks the sky.
That's why
I'll meet it in our river again someday,
that very drop of water –
I hope we will then greet each other.

The Maple Flame

The blaze of sunlit birches
the flame of maples
rooting in still waters
are by-products of
pigment breakdown,
grown-ups say.

The richness of our autumns
yellow – bright yellow – purple – red
are the result of
poor thin soil,
the feast of Scarlet Oak and Sassafras,
of Tamarack and Eastern Sycamore
highlights the end of growth,
grown-ups say.

No doubt
the leaves will fall.
Yet they descend
in serene beauty,
the sunlit birch
the maple flame.

Birch Shower

Did you ever see
      the
         rain
  that
          dro
   ps
from a ripe birch tree
on a sunny Monday morning?

The sky is wide
the air is clear
from a crisp blue night
with frost around the corner.

In the first light
the leaves come free,
yellow and bright,
keep rolling from their branches.

No wind and no sound
then a rustle and a bustle
flakes dance to the ground
to be quiet, all quiet again…

A short magic spell,
a brief golden shower,
yet you can tell
the star coins are clinking!

A beautiful blessing –
Then, one by one
     by
        one
    by
        one
the leaves
    have gone
        on.

Leaf diving

When the fireworks of autumn colors
are all gone
I like to stay
and saunter through thick tiers of foliage.
I hear the swish and rustle
while I drag my feet
and search for one last yellow leaf
or a flaming red one not yet withered
not yet crumbling into soil
and humbly making room for cold and winter.
There are not many days remaining
for noisy walks through foliage
all dry and brittle
and light like feathers in the wind.
I throw some leaves high up into the air
and they sink unhurried
to the ground - a dreamlike rain.
I heap the leaves onto the forest floor
and then I dive headlong into the earthy huddle
as if I never would come out again.

Angels
in the Backwoods

The Cat With No Hat

Raggyns, my cat,
he has no hat.
He has no coat and no purse,
and what's much worse:
He has no manners whatsoever.
(Yet he thinks of himself
as frightfully clever).

What shall I do about that:
a beast with no hat
no tux and no glove?
(It is – after all – the cat I love.)

Making

Wow! all that white white snow!
Raggyns and I are making tracks:
BIG BOOT tracks and
PAD PAD PAD PAD tracks.

BIG BOOT
PAD PAD PAD PAD

BIG BIG BIG
I'm jumping on one foot,
while Rags goes
PAD PAD   PAD PAD
PAD PAD   PAD PAD

And then he goes after
teeny tiny teeny tiny bird tracks.

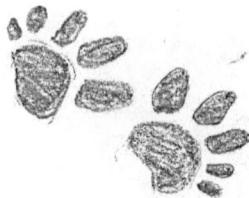

Tracks

Faster and faster they both go:
PAD PAD   teeny tiny   teeny tiny
PAD PAD   teeny tiny   teeny tiny

No! I cry, Raggyns come back!!
And I run after cat and bird
through the deep white snow.
BIG BOOT PAD PAD teeny tiny

All at once
there are no more bird tracks.
None. Just BIG BOOT and
PAD PAD PAD PAD.

High up on the tree
I hear a Chickadee jeer.

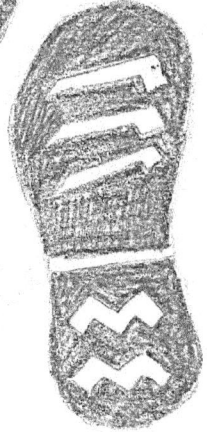

North Pole Around the Corner

North Pole
lies just around the corner
for the more far-seeing mind
of us little folks.

My cat turns into an arctic lynx
I live in an igloo-tent
or in an Indian tipi
covered with heavy snow.

The squirrels leave big tracks like Bear.
Black "eagles" landing everywhere
to catch their prey,
that is, crumbs from our dinner table…

…which reminds me
tea and cake are ready
for us weary travelers now
a short way from North Pole,
at a warm place called home.

Father Bear

Father Bear, he is so slow…
He rather tries my patience –
although it's no surprise, you know,
he's on his way to hibernation.

I Built a Snowman!

Today I built a snowman!
A snowman big and round.
His eyes are jet-black pebbles,
his nose 's a pine cone I just found.

A row of nuts he has for teeth
His arms are made of sticks
His hair grows oh so evergreen.
He needs no hat, no scarf, no mitts.

Snowman is rather splendid
I do like him a lot
I wish he would stay with me
even when it gets hot.

Squirrel's Quest

Squirrel cannot find
the nuts and cones she put in store!
(Never mind
She's lost them many times before.)

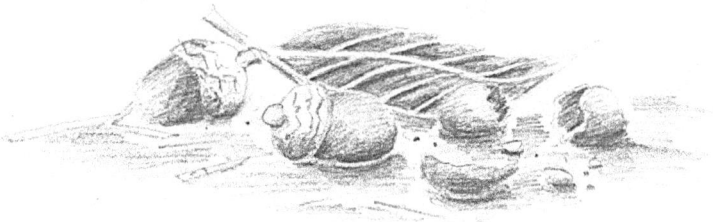

Snowflakes Dancing

Snowflakes dancing twisting twirling
fast and faster through the air
Snowflakes spinning wild and wilder
racing, chasing without care.

Snowflakes falling falling falling
piling on the smallest tree
whitening woods and fields and bolders,
the tiny black cap of Chickadee.

Snowflakes dancing twisting twirling
tumbling steadily from the sky
make the world quite small and silent
- all you hear is one big sigh.

Angels in the Backwoods

That pure white snow!
Let's be off and go
be the first to make a track
lie down flat on our back.

Look out, Rags!
I move my hands sideways
my feet sideways
and scream and shout.

And laugh!
Laugh at the angel high above
who's merry too and looking down
on me and my angelic gown,
the flurry of those moving feet
where heaven and earth and children meet.

Happy Birthday, Green Forest!

I know my birthday
and Rags' birthday I know too.
I know when Groundhog, Owl and Otter
celebrate their feast each year.
Yet I do not know at all
when Green Forest saw the light of day.
Is his birthdate in deep winter
when all trees wear diadems of snow and ice?
Was Forest born in early spring
when buds and blossoms
weave a festive gown?
Should we celebrate in summertime
when berries red and blue are ripe
all ready for a cake?
Or is his date of birth in fall
when every leaf contributes
to a firework of brilliant colors?
I do not know, I can't find out
so every day I visit in the woods I say:
Happy Birthday, Green Forest,
Happy Birthday to you!

Priceless Rainbow

At the end of the rainbow
you will find a pot of gold,
so they say, the story is quite old.
But I don't want to find that treasure
and measure
the price of Rainbow's splendor
(anyway, who'd be the vendor?)
The promise in each Rainbow
is not for sale.

What I Love

I love Big Moon and Silver Star
they are so old, so wise, so far

I love the gentle touch of Mother
so close and warm, and I love Father

I love the Wind swaying tall blades of grass
and rippling water, breaking it like glass

I love Rags, my cat,
though he pretends he's callous
(I think he sometimes is just jealous)

I love Sun who makes us bright and gay
and warms the ponds so we can play

I love my friend the cheerful Otter
who rides with me the teeter-totter

I love Rain, who softly sprays the land
so plants can grow and lives expand

I love Squirrel although she's rather fussy -
I guess that's simply what she must be

I love all four Seasons as they come and go
and show me things I didn't know.

You can read more of Ailinn, Raggyns and
their friends of Green Forest in the following
two storybooks:

The Song that Green Forest Sang
Ailinn's Adventures in Green Forest, Volume 1
Written by Robert W. Griffin
Illustrations by Elizabeth Auer

What is Never Lost
Ailinn's Adventures in Green Forest, Volume 2
Written by Robert W. Griffin
Illustrations by Elizabeth Auer

Lotta Suter

is a journalist, translator and book author, currently working as an US correspondent for various media in Switzerland and Germany. In her long career as a writer she has penned and translated political essays and nonfiction works for adults as well as many stories and poems for children and the young at heart. Among her works are the libretti for the three chamber operas *Yona*, *Sarai* and *Ruwth* to which her husband Robert Griffin composed the music. She lives with Robert, her dog, her cat and her chickens in the foothills of the Swiss Alps.

Elizabeth Auer

is an artist and illustrator and currently teaches art and handwork at Oxbow Schoolhouse in Devens, Mass. She has also taught many courses in the arts to adults, including watercolor painting, clay modeling and drawing. She is the author and illustrator of *Creative Pathways* and *Learning To See the World through Drawing*, both published by Waldorf Publications. Chatham, NY

www.ingramcontent.com/pod-product-compliance
Lightning Source LLC
Chambersburg PA
CBHW060947040426

42445CB00011B/1038